INTERPRETING THE
PROPHETIC

INTERPRETING THE
PROPHETIC

MAKING THE MOST OF GOD'S
WORDS AND PROMISES

MARC BRISEBOIS

INTERPRETING THE PROPHETIC
Copyright © 2016 Watchman Publishing

For more information regarding permissions to reproduce material from this book, please email or write:

Watchman on the Wall Ministries
Box 3458, Spruce Grove, AB, Canada
T7X 3A7

info@watchman.ca

ISBN: 0-9868299-4-3
ISBN-13: 978-0-9868299-4-9

Printed by CreateSpace, An Amazon.com Company
Available from Amazon.com and other retail outlets

Dedication

I wish to dedicate this work to the many prophetic voices who, over the years, modelled both the methodology as well as the heart of the Kingdom of God in their ministry. Like a fly on the wall I participated in your journey by watching and learning with you as you ventured out to fulfill the call of God on your lives.

Acknowledgements

A special thanks to all who helped with the production process. Of particular note are the members of our editing team who invested countless hours. Thank you Marie Spenst, Wendy Brisebois, Nicole Martineau, Laverne Kundert and Murray MacKinnon.

Endorsements

Marc gives us clear and timely insights into the prophetic ministry from years of experience in the local church and globally. Those who read this book will greatly benefit from Marc's journey, and avoid the pitfalls that so often come with the Prophetic realm. A must read for those just starting to venture into the prophetic, and those who have been walking in Prophetic ministry for years.

David Demian
Watchmen for the Nations

If you want to embrace the prophetic gift at a much higher level, or have been affected by the misuse of this kingdom office you need this book. Marc challenges you to either rethink or broaden your understanding as to how the prophetic should be delivered and interpreted.

"Interpreting The Prophetic" is in sync with a global intent to revisit, if not redefine, the original design and purpose of the prophetic process for releasing spiritual insight and foresight to God's people. In addition, Marc addresses the diverse styles of the prophetic office. Especially enjoyable is the distinction between Old Covenant and New Covenant, so often blurred. His unique emphasis on the corporate is in line with our progression toward spiritual maturity and capitalizes on the importance of the prophetic as a supernatural effort to unify the people of God.

Currently, God is shifting the body of Christ into a greater sphere of governmental influence on the earth. Since the days of Moses until now, the office of the prophet and the prophetic gift have served to propel the people of God into their eternal purpose. The labor of time and love that has been invested in this book will exhort you and motivate you to do just that.

Michael Danforth
Founder of Mountain Top International
School Of Higher Learning

Prophetic utterance is one of the most helpful gifts the Lord has given His church to fulfill her destiny. It is also at times one of the most misunderstood and misapplied. Marc Brisebois comes with a solid experience both as an international prophet and church leader to bring clarity that is so needed. In a simple and practical way, he gives us the essentials we need to rightly interpret the prophetic. This book is a must for whoever wants to give or receive a Prophetic Word. We're making it a mandatory read to our apostolic network!

Alain Caron
Hodos Network

I appreciate the way Marc explains prophetic gifting—both as a prophet, and as one who receives Prophetic Words. He is very balanced and Biblical, but also writes from personal experience which makes for interesting reading.

I commend Marc for who he is and for his prophetic gift for the body of Christ.

Donna Ruth Jordan
YWAM Associates International

There are many opportunities and potential dangers that believers face regularly in their christian walk. One of the great gifts to the body of Christ is "governments" (1 Corinthians 12:28). Marc functions in this gifting... Steering and navigating for us in choppy waters, so that we can find safety and blessing in the calmer, deeper waters out there.

Apostle Doug Schneider

Table of Contents

Foreword

Thank you Marc for taking the time to share your knowledge and experience in learning the proper principles for "Interpreting the Prophetic".

I am very careful about endorsing material on the prophetic. I have been an advocate for the prophetic since I first started prophesying in 1952 – 64 years ago. I became more prophetic in 1973 when I had the divine visitation that activated me into an unlimited prophetic flow. During the following years to the present I personally have prophesied over 50,000 individuals. In 1988 the Prophetic Movement was birthed at our 2nd International Gathering of Prophets.

In 1984 an old prophet prophesied that God was giving me the anointing to be a reproducer reproducing reproducers who reproduce. I wrote three books on prophets and personal prophecy. And then in 1989 I wrote a 300 page manual for teaching, activating and training saints and ordained ministers. To the present date we have trained over 250,000 Christians in every continent to be prophetic.

I revealed all of this to let readers know I have a zeal for the integrity of the prophetic. So when someone like Marc Brisebois writes a book on "Interpreting the Prophetic" I want to make sure he has presented proper principles, the attitude for the prophesier, willing to be taught, corrected and a strong desire to be more accurate and minister prophetically where it is honoring to Jesus and gives glory to God.

I can say that the principles for interpreting and ministering the prophetic that you present are scriptural and good things for saints to know and practice.

I could list many other principle and practices for the prophetic but that is not the purpose of this Foreword. It is to let you know that a senior Prophet that is recognized in most parts of the world as the Father of the Prophetic Movement gives confirmation that you can read and practice with confidence the contents of this book.

God bless you Marc for writing this book. I can tell it is not just head knowledge and book learning, but written from personal knowledge and growing and adjusting through life experience. Every person desiring to be prophetic needs to read this book.

Bishop Bill Hamon
Bishop of Christian International Apostolic Network

Author: The Eternal Church, Prophets & Personal Prophecy, Prophets & the Prophetic Movement, Prophets, Pitfalls, & Principles, Apostles/Prophets & the Coming Moves of God, The Day of the Saints, Who Am I & Why Am I here, Prophetic Scriptures Yet to be Fulfilled, 70 Reasons for Speaking in Tongues, and How Can These Things Be?

Introduction

Prophetic ministry is complicated at best. Until the Kingdom of Heaven is fully realized and we stand in His actual presence, we will always see through a glass darkly (1 Corinthians 13:12). We need to become comfortable with the reality that some elements of interpreting the prophetic will continue to be challenging. Even so, there are a few keys we can learn along the way which will help us. This book is an effort to provide some assistance and even possibly, enlightenment to the reader.

The Domain of God

At the core of interpretation is the fact that all interpretation belongs to God. Joseph demonstrated his grasp of this concept while imprisoned. When asked by the King's butler and baker to interpret some distressing dreams, Joseph immediately responds saying, *"Do not interpretations belong to God?"* (Genesis 40:8).

Not only does this mean we need to lean on God for wisdom, but it suggests limitations to the prophetic voices God will use in our lives. Prophetic Words and ministry will not always be perfectly clear. Furthermore, prophets are not omniscient. They do not know everything about your life, a fact which should not diminish their legitimacy. This is one way you can identify an immature prophetic voice; those who need to make themselves indispensable are driven by ego. Mature ones, on the other hand, shy away from the pressure of your misplaced expectations.

At the same time God will use all sorts. Inexperienced prophets are in training and God will also use them to speak to us. It is important to be gracious and patient as you would any child developing a new skill. Just do not be taken in by immaturity or the ambitious. Remember, only God possesses ALL knowledge. He dispenses that knowledge through vessels, but at His own discretion and to the degree the vessel itself can handle it.

Each prophetic voice God uses, from the novice believer to the mature seasoned seer, must operate within the boundary of certain limitations. Even Elijah faced circumstances where he was effectively blind/deaf. Though at times he walked in so much knowledge it seemed nothing was hid from him, there were moments when he could not see clearly. This was certainly the case when God was dealing with him on a personal level (1 Kings 19). He was as unsure about what God was saying as we can be. Even in the context of his National ministry, he was also at times limited.

The Place of Love

Despite this fact prophets can still be intimidating. Learning to deal with this element can itself lead to mistakes. The greater the authority and gift, the more other people may misread their motives and behaviour. It is not easy knowing how to behave when you sense someone knows all about your life. Particularly, if you feel your failures are exposed, it is natural to want to hide. Feeling defensive is not the answer nor is finding fault. Rather there are two points in our stance which are critical. The one is realizing prophetic voices do NOT know all, which we have addressed already. The other is resting in the comfort provided in knowing mature prophets are driven by love.

This is very difficult to keep in mind particularly if we feel under condemnation, but can still be done.

It begins by believing the best. For example you can start by trusting that mature believers do not look with eyes of disapproval. Even when they are bringing correction or challenges, it is never to vilify or demean. Like a parent disciplining their child, it is corrective, not punitive and ultimately, for the good of the child.

So learn to relax around prophetic ministers. Realize mature prophets have been where you are and do not easily forget. Even if they see you in your imperfection, they will not perceive you negatively. Weakness to the mature, is not failure. It would be like watching a 2 year old trying to do what they have never done. Is there anyone who can't treasure the effort of a tenacious toddler? They are not less just because they are 2 and not 3 years old.

This kind of thinking is the product of prideful paranoia. Love does not see the 2 year old from the perspective of what they are unable to do. Like mothers and fathers, you simply enjoy the moments and the beauty of who they are in the moment.

Love is the foundation from which every ministry gift must be launched. Whatever gifts or abilities God gives, it is for the sole purpose of transforming us into the likeness of Christ. Similarly the words and promises God is giving you are designed to bring you into your destiny. At the end of the day, this is the perspective we need to take when viewing and interpreting the prophetic. The goal and heart of God is that we might grow into the kinds of people He has already seen we can become. And so as we move into our first chapter, we get a glimpse of God's redemptive heart. While God does correct and judge, His motive is always to bring blessing and increase.

Chapter 1

Consider the Skinny Cows

Interpreting Prophetic Words can be a tricky business. Often we approach Prophetic Words in a fatalistic way with a punitive God in mind. However, Prophetic Words often only point to events and possibilities without ever uncovering God's purpose or will. Imagine if Joseph had taken this approach concerning Pharaoh's dreams of the skinny and fat cows. If the dreams of Pharaoh had been viewed as the intention of God, Egypt would have been left to destruction. Instead, Joseph saw it not as the end of the world, but as an opportunity to change the world.

The Dreams

Pharaoh had two dreams which effectively said the same thing. The message in them was to say there would be seven years of plenty (fat cows) followed by seven years of famine (the skinny cows). Joseph did not interpret the dreams with the mindset that God was bent on the destruction of Egypt. Even though God does judge nations, Joseph did not automatically read that into the message. Apparently it was not God's intention at the time and Joseph did not assume 'judgment' going in. As we all know, eventually God did judge Egypt, but that was much later.

Instead Joseph saw an alternative. The fact that there was even an alternative tells us something about prophetic interpretation. His attitude gives us insight into one of the purposes of prophecy.

First he indicates the dreams are from God. This is a vital first step before we attempt to discern the message. Is it or is it not from God? Determining the answer to this question is not always easy. In this case, Joseph quickly determined the dream to have come from God. God is clearly telling Pharaoh what He (God) is about to do. What is unusual is that Joseph saw these warnings as a gesture of mercy and not necessarily a threat.

Here is Joseph's take:

"And the dream was repeated to Pharaoh twice because the thing is established by God, and God will shortly bring it to pass."
(Genesis 41:32)

In passing we should note this particular aspect of interpretation. Joseph immediately understood repetition to be significant. This is not a matter of interpretation so much as it is an aspect of knowledge. We have no idea where Joseph discovered this principle but evidently it was part of his grid for prophetic dreams. From this point Joseph moves into the next phase of interpretation which is strategic wisdom! This is certainly the rarest commodity in this field.

The Apostolic Interpretation

Joseph does not even think to interpret this dream as the express purpose of God. Otherwise he would have thrown his hands in the air in resignation. Instead he immediately proposes a solution, effectively averting the consequences of the famine. How many of us would have gone there? No, we usually interpret the prophetic as an expression of the will of God.

This is partially because of our misunderstanding of the prophetic and because we do not know the love of God. Our default starting point is the punitive approach we secretly believe God holds.

We view God as vindictive and always punitive and so instinctively think *'inevitable destruction'*. Remember, that was never God's intention here, nor was it God's heart when he sent Jonah to Nineveh.

This is not to say God's warnings do not involve His wrath. Remember when He spoke to Moses about destroying Israel. Though He was angry He really wanted to show mercy. Moses' intercession brought out the mercy of God. Likewise here, the warnings of God create an opportunity for mercy. Joseph knew this and so moved into a redemptive interpretation.

> ***"Now therefore, let Pharaoh select a discerning and wise man and set him over the land of Egypt."***
> (Genesis 41:33)

The key here is around understanding or misunderstanding the purpose of God. Knowing the nature of God can help us discern His intention. We often forget that God is long-suffering; far more long-suffering than we are. Often it is our own egos, relishing the opportunity to be vindicated, which blind us from God's actual design.

When we receive a message such as these dreams, there are a number of directions we could take. Assuming God is determined to destroy Egypt would have been an easy response. The underlying implication is *'no amount of supply will be enough'*. In effect, the land will be consumed. Many might have interpreted this to be a time to 'run and hide'. Moreover, if it is God, who are we to resist His will?

Joseph had the good sense to realize God's notifications, while dire, were not conclusive or an unfolding of manifest destiny. So while there are limits to God's patience, His intention is not to destroy us, but to change our hearts or cause us to modify our behavior. Even a harsh Word is meant to turn the heart to repentance so He can show mercy.

Agabus

The New Testament gives us another example of this kind of backward interpretation. Actually, what we see is a complete misinterpretation by everyone except Paul. The scenario unfolds with a prophet named Agabus visiting Paul and others in the city of Caesarea. While with Paul, Agabus gives him a Prophetic Word saying he would be arrested and put in jail.

In this case the others felt it was a warning with options before them. In other words, *"Paul, do not continue on your journey to Jerusalem."* This was the interpretation of the entire group.

"And when we heard these things, both we, and they of that place, besought him not to go up to Jerusalem. Then Paul

> *answered, 'What mean you to weep and to break mine heart? for I am ready not to be bound only, but also to die at Jerusalem for the name of the Lord Jesus.' And when he would not be persuaded, we ceased, saying, 'The will of the Lord be done.'"*
>
> (Acts 21:12-14)

Although initially resistant, in the end they resigned themselves to the will of God. Once again, the perceived will of God is what guided their interpretation. However, Paul was already convinced of his purpose and that he would testify not only before Jerusalem, but also in Rome. This was later confirmed when the angel of the Lord appeared to him.

> *"For there stood by me this night an angel of the God to whom I belong and whom I serve, saying, 'Do not be afraid, Paul; you must be brought before Caesar;'"*
>
> (Acts 27:23-24)

The best interpretations in both of these instances hinged on either a knowledge of the heart of God or a specific understanding of His purposes. It was not about going to Jerusalem or not, nor being arrested or not, but the intent of God. Interpretation is largely hindered when we know neither God's purpose nor the fullness of His intention for us.

In the example of Joseph, who through strategic wisdom and knowing the heart of God, a potential loss is turned into a great win for Egypt. For Paul, the Prophetic Word was a confirmation of his future. As it was, only he understood the purpose for which God was taking him to Jerusalem.

All this is not to say that God will not judge nations. Nor does it mean we must submit to imprisonment or persecution. Rather there is intention and purpose equal to the moment. While not always easily discerned, there are clear postures which can hinder our ability to see clearly. Our view of God is one of those factors which will define our approach. Seeing God as punitive and angry will definitely cast a shadow. It may be that the better part of learning to interpret is found in diminishing our ego and crafting a better perspective of the heart of God.

What He really wants is for us to learn His heart and adjust our course towards Him. Remembering, that He makes the rain to fall on the righteous and the unrighteous, it is important we see His desire to redeem. He longs for all mankind to be saved and it is His deepest desire that we experience life abundantly. As such, both Paul's and Joseph's actions and words represent an accurate and healthy response to heaven's prophetic warning.

Chapter 2

Intention and Meaning

If we are going to Interpret the Prophetic we should have a working understanding of some of the ways God uses mankind. Sometimes it is easy to elevate someone who seems to know secrets about our lives. Yet, God has a sense of humor and a keen ability to show man his limitations. This becomes clear in moments of prophecy when the intention of the speaker and the meaning to the hearer differ immensely.

The Prophetic Voice

God never meant for prophetic voices to have all the answers for the minutia of our lives. If this is not clear to us now, it will be once we realize men know and prophesy in part. This can become clear in a number of ways. Scripture certainly reveals this fact. It is demonstrated in the life of one of the most eminent prophetic voices of the Old Testament.

Elisha had been hosted by a Shunammite woman who set up a room to provide for Elisha along his journey. He wanted to bless her and discovered she had no son. Elisha then prophesied over her that she would bear a son within the year, which she did. However, the boy later died and then, while traumatized, she came to Elisha. When his servant Gehazi would have put her away, Elisha realized something important had been hidden from him.

> *"Now when she came to the man of God at the hill, she caught him by the feet, but Gehazi came near to push her away. But the man of God said, 'Let her alone; for her soul is in deep distress, and the Lord <u>has hidden it from me</u>, and has not told me.'"*
> (2 Kings 4:27)

This is a classic example of the limitations God puts on men. What is clear is that the legitimacy of a prophetic gift is not determined by the "all-knowing" calibre of the prophet. At times He will even use a donkey to get things done. This does not validate the donkey as much as it glorifies God.

At the same time diversity and calibre of gifting is significant. God will distinguish between levels of gifting in order to give men the reason and means to submit and honor. That is, in order to create a hierarchy of authority he gives more to one and less to another. This applies to wisdom, musical talent, faith, technical prowess, etc.; essentially all levels of gifting, no matter the sphere. The key is to realize **we all** operate well below omniscient.

This is echoed in the New Testament model of gifts. Paul, in writing about the operation of the gifts of the Spirit, says as much when he wrote, *"For we know in part and we prophesy in part"* (1 Corinthians 13:9). We should never be surprised at our own ignorance or the limitations on even the most gifted.

Diversity of Administrations

Another aspect of the prophetic ministry is the diversity of styles and administration of the gifts. This has to do with the way in which some minister. For example, some prophesy from a point of understanding, whereas others prophesy out of faith to the point where they have absolutely no insight on what they are saying. Those who move from knowledge have a clear view of the circumstances of people's lives and can speak with a fuller awareness of the context of what God might be doing. Others may have no awareness of the context of the situation and yet can be incredibly accurate in their gifting.

These speak from a place of pure faith and Holy Spirit unction. Those who operate by unction might refer to this as a 'bubbling-up' kind of inspiration. This means they can deliver a clear Prophetic Word without having a lot of insight on the circumstances of the person receiving the Word. This can be confusing as they appear to have more specific insight than they do. These, by all appearances, seem to know precise details of a person's life, and yet after, when they are asked to elaborate, have nothing other than what they were inspired to say. This is not unusual and again does not negate the value or legitimacy of what was shared.

What this suggests is there are different administrations of grace and we need to be careful who we are leaning on for clarity. We would not want to put undue pressure on God's servant to move past the grace of his or her gift. Neither would we want to minimize the Word based on whether we think they knew what they were talking about.

Caiaphas

This was certainly the case with the High Priest of Israel. As the inquisition against Jesus approached, the Pharisees and Sadducees were livid. Attempting to avert the effect of a series of Jesus' amazing miracles, they considered how to nullify Him. They were in chaos, fearing the loss of political and social authority. People were turning en masse to Jesus and something had to be done.

As they gathered the High Priest made the most astounding declaration.

> *"And one of them, Caiaphas, being high priest that year, said to them, 'You know nothing at all, nor do you consider that it is expedient for us that one man should die for the people, and not that the whole nation should perish.'"*
> (John 11:49-50)

Now this man was no friend of Jesus, neither was he in the counsel of God. Rather, being completely oblivious to the significance of what he was saying, he articulates the divine intent of God. However, he does it with malice and murder as his motive. What is even more surprising is the next verse.

> *"Now this he did not say on his own authority; but being high priest that year he prophesied that Jesus would die for the nation,"*
> (John 11:51)

Despite the fact that his intentions were entirely evil and that he was not purposely moving in the prophetic, he prophesied. It does not change the message itself, but it has a bearing on how we see the vessel delivering this Word. For starters the character of the individual does not necessarily define the reliability of the Word. Obviously this is a rare and odd circumstance. However, it does open up the possibility of it happening again. That is, the prophetic voice can think one thing and the Holy Spirit intend another. Personally I have had many such moments, not with evil motives, but simply from a place of ignorance. Here is one vivid example.

My Experience

A number of years ago, during my first visit to Guatemala, I spoke in a church. I did not know the pastor of the church, who has since become a very good friend, but was greatly blessed by the atmosphere. As typically happens before I minister, I was getting a great deal of inspiration from the worship.

It was as if their prayers were calling for and releasing rain over the region. Their worship was opening the heavens and a deluge of water was being poured out on the city. It was incredibly vivid. I've had this often before and most times it signifies the church is a Gatekeeper Church and is acting through their worship in an intercessory fashion.

On this occasion there was an amazing richness to the atmosphere. I was overwhelmed with the blessing I felt being released into the city. When I got up to speak, I was so captivated with these thoughts, I forgot to introduce myself or say anything about our ministry. I just began to bless them as a church and prophetically tell them what they were doing in the Spirit.

From there, I went right into speaking about the apostolic nature of some churches, including this one, and how it was meant to bless the city. It was then that I realized the pastor in the front row was literally sobbing. As I looked down tears were streaming from his face and his body was in near convulsions, he was so affected. At the time I wondered what was specifically affecting him, though it was obvious the atmosphere was still electrically charged. Little did I know his story.

Later, during lunch, he shared his testimony with me. I was shocked when I discovered the actual reason he was weeping. The Holy Spirit had been speaking to him about his city and he longed to make a great impact. He had been told to anoint the city with water, which he had never done before. That is, he was to literally hire a water truck and go around the city anointing the city with water. It was a strange and somewhat unusual initiative for him.

But that very morning, at 5am, he and some other leaders had gone around their city praying and anointing the city with water. Imagine how blessed he was when the first words out of my mouth were the following: "The water that you've poured out today will prove to be a great blessing to the city."

Application

Here is the difference between intention and meaning. While I was envisioning something spiritual and intangible, he heard God speak to him about his obedience. It was not necessary for me to know anything about what he had done that morning to speak prophetically. Although I meant those words for the immediate context, it did not matter.

Though I saw in part, the value of the words were the same as was evident in his response. Had he asked me about my intention, it would not have matched his experience. His experience was far more literal than my prophetic vision. However, what I saw still validated what he had done and fulfilled God's prophetic intent. This is the way the Holy Spirit knits together miraculous moments without anyone but Him getting the credit.

Chapter 3

The New Testament Shift

When it comes to prophetic ministry there are fundamental differences between Old and New Testament. The shift that takes place between the covenants is important to note. While prophetic ministry remains critical to both covenants, our relationship to the Holy Spirit differs significantly. Therefore our expectations of the Holy Spirit at work in others, as well as ourselves, will differ.

In vs Upon

The key difference has to do with the juxtaposition of the Holy Spirit in us, as opposed to coming upon us. The Old Testament saints were as yet unredeemed and required a kind of buffer or separation. This reality is reflected in the imagery of the temple with its separate compartments. The actual presence of God was in the 3rd inner compartment where only the High Priest could enter once a year. This ceremony was dangerous, as any missed protocols could mean his instantaneous death.

At the moment of Jesus' death, the curtain was torn between the Holy of Holies and the Holy place. This symbolized the end of this era. Despite their faith and obedience, Old Testament prophets were not born again and therefore not afforded the access we have today. The idea that we become one with God's Spirit is a unique level of intertwining which did not previously exist. We are now one spirit with God.

> *"But he who is joined to the Lord is one spirit with Him."*
> (1 Corinthians 6:17)

The implications of this amazing truth are many! Among them is the fact that the Holy Spirit came **upon** them, but did not dwell **in** them. This is part of the significance of Jesus as Immanuel, which is to say 'God with us'. Again, it is the same reason why the Apostle Paul writes we are the temple of the Holy Spirit (1 Corinthians 6:19). But this was certainly not the case with Old Testament saints.

The Mechanics of Yielding

Today's believer is required to cooperate and yield to the Holy Spirit. This was not part of the equation in the Old Covenant. Instead, the Holy Spirit would come upon a person and essentially assume complete control. The margin for error in those cases was zero and so was their measure for true and false prophets.

This wholesale approach is far simpler but makes man a mere conduit. The individual's functional role is reduced to vessel. While this served His purpose, it does not really represent God's intent for us today. Alternatively, we are partners with God and are required to use discernment concerning the Spirit's work and guidance. We are called co-heirs and co-workers.

This union with God creates a scenario where we are not coerced into obeying or releasing the Spirit of God. The gifts of the Spirit are subject to our will and it is within our purview to be used or not. At what level God uses us is within His jurisdiction, but we must make ourselves willing and available. We choose when to prophesy and also to prophesy according to our capacity of hearing and discerning.

In the Corinthian church when some of the saints decided to act like Old Testament believers they were rebuked. These had started speaking and prophesying at random intervals as though it was not in their power to withhold. Paul was essentially saying you are not being forced to act out these prophetic things, that is an old pattern. Instead he advised them as follows:

> *"And the spirits of the prophets are subject to the prophets."*
> (1 Corinthians 14:32)

The confusion created by random manifestations was not necessary. We have the Holy Spirit in us and in cooperation with our will, He is released with consent. The yielding component was entirely new to the Corinthians and took some adjusting. It did make the prophetic ministry more subject to error as so much depends on us. This is why Paul told them that when one prophesies, the others should judge. However, no stonings were required, only moments of exhortation and training.

Currently then, we must discriminate between our own thoughts and God's leading. The margin for error is much greater. This should have great bearing on how we evaluate New Testament prophetic ministry. If you apply the Old Testament standard no one would survive – the penalty was death!

A Closer Look

To really drive this home we should take a closer look at the Old Testament model. Not much of the Old Testament writings were instructional so there is not a lot of descriptive language. Still, there are inferences to be made. In the case of Saul, the king of Israel, we see moments when he prophesied and was accounted to be among the prophets. This happened twice in his life that we know of, and gives us a vital perspective.

Firstly, when Saul meets the prophet Samuel, he is given a Word about becoming the king. He is also given some very specific instructions that God would change his heart and that he would meet a school of Prophets. This happened and the Spirit of God fell on him so that he prophesied. This is when the proverb begins concerning Saul.

> *"Then a man from there answered and said, 'But who is their father?' Therefore it became a proverb: 'Is Saul also among the prophets?'"*
> (1 Samuel 10:12)

The second time happens later in his life when he begins to stray from God. An evil spirit begins to oppress him and he recruits David to drive the spirits away from him. Eventually even David's music is unable to bring him comfort. This signifies a greater level of demonization as the evil spirit seems to stay with Saul. When the Spirit of God falls on him again, he prophesies just like the first time.

There is one notable difference. Instead of merely prophesying he tears off his clothes and lies on the ground naked day and night. Why? Because when the Spirit of God comes on him he is torn inwardly, being already demonized by a spirit. These two do not mix well together. The Spirit of God, being irresistible and far more powerful, dominates. The evil spirit fights in vain, wrestling in a tormented fashion in an attempt to maintain supremacy.

> *"So he went there to Naioth in Ramah. Then the Spirit of God was upon him also, and he went on and prophesied until he came to Naioth in Ramah. And he also stripped off his clothes and prophesied before Samuel in like manner, and lay down naked all that day and all that night. Therefore they say, 'Is Saul also among the prophets?'"*
> (1 Samuel 19:23-24)

Clearly the first experience was not exactly like the second.

The torment is a reflection of the manner in which the Holy Spirit came on Old Testament believers. Today things are very different. A Word can be true in degrees. It also suggests that we must exercise patience with one another while we give room for growth.

Accuracy in Increments

A simple example of this is seen in the ministry of Agabus in Caesarea. Here the prophet joins Paul and his party at the house of Philip who had four daughters who were also prophets. Agabus gives him a Word which is generally correct but not really 100%.

> *"When he had come to us, he took Paul's hands and feet, and said, 'Thus says the Holy Spirit, So shall the Jews at Jerusalem bind the man who owns this belt, and deliver him into the hands of the Gentiles.'"*
> (Acts 21:11)

The actual story played out slightly different; it was the Roman soldiers doing the binding. Nevertheless the heart of the message was correct. In the end it is not about absolute certainty. This is required only by those who seek to nullify or disprove the prophetic. We should simply understand the difference in the role of the Holy Spirit in the New Covenant. Faith has the boldness to venture and experiment, even if it means some mistakes are made along the way. What is most critical is the development of our faith and our capacity to yield. As it matures it will manifest a clearer expression of God.

Chapter 4

The Corporate Nature of Prophecy

One of the purposes of Prophetic Words is to encourage us towards our destiny. However we have a habit of using them to elevate ourselves beyond God's intention. The same language used to create value can be used to bolster a kind of elitist view of ourselves. Then when others fail to comprehend our importance we resent them. Here is an approach that can help us avoid doing this. As a general rule we should view our roles and destinies as part of the collective Body of Christ instead of stand alone parts.

Consider An Engine

Imagine the Body of Christ as a vehicle with an engine instead of a body. Every part is important, but some parts are more essential than others. Yet, let it be clear, they all matter. The Prophetic Word is meant to isolate the importance of the parts and motivate them to fulfill their purpose. It is not intended to separate us from the whole. That, unfortunately, is frequently how we lose our essential purpose.

Let's illustrate this by seeing ourselves as an engine part instead of a body part. Pretend you are a metal rod inside a combustion engine. Knowing the inner workings of a combustion engine is helpful but not entirely necessary. So for now think of yourself as just a metal rod not yet fitted into an engine.

As a metal rod you have a sense of purpose but do not know your place in the world. Then the Prophetic Word comes to your life. It might sound something like this:

"Thus says the Lord you are a rod of God's purpose. Before you were created I knew you and destined you to stand in a special and distinct place. I will use you in a powerful way. I will move in you with unusual speed and in a prepared place. You will be strengthened to bear weight and I will move you to shift my people from one place to another. I will shape you to fit in that unique place and will temper you to glorify Me as the power of My Spirit will

move through you. And you will be in many places serving My purpose and divine intention."

This is a great Word and it is very encouraging. Taken as a whole one should immediately realize there is no value in trying to fulfill this. No amount of doing anything a rod might be able to do will help attain destiny. Rather, the aim of this kind of exhortation is meant to increase our desire to function properly. It imparts faith and hope for the future. However what we hear and what was said can vary immensely. So what does it really mean?

Before we answer that question we should say what it does not mean. Often when we get a Prophetic Word we try to interpret it in the context of our present life. In relationship to this simple metal rod, nothing in it's past can give context for it's future. Unless it has already operated as part of an engine it will very likely misinterpret by looking to the past to define the future. This is a common mistake. So now we ask again, 'what does it mean?'

The Manufacturing Process

For starters this Word points to a process which will prepare the rod for its place. There is a great tendency to skip this part, and yet it represents the bulk of time between the present and the future promise.

Process should not be undervalued. This means when the Spirit of God says *'you will be strengthened'*, it signifies the removal of weakness. Sometimes we hear terms like these and do not realize they are not incidental. There is more than meets the eye in this single word. Our growth is always about death and resurrection, as we decrease and He increases. This process may be very unpleasant and difficult at times, but utterly necessary.

Similarly when the Spirit refers to *'shaping us'*, He is pointing to a process. This involves the chastening of the Lord which prepares us to stand in our place and function as participants in His Holy plan (Hebrews 12:7-11). Much can be said about this! It is especially important since this passage indicates we cannot be partakers of His Holiness without this discipline. In the case of Paul the Spirit explicitly added, *'I will show him how many things he must suffer'* (Acts 9:16). Destiny can never be divorced from journey.

Going back to our engine illustration we can imagine what kinds of processes are involved in manufacturing engine parts. It could mean subjecting the metal to heat for prolonged periods and possibly cutting off the length so it is the right size. Then we may need to add components to each end of the rod so it can become attached to the rest of the engine. All of this is surprising as it was not what we expected, but is necessary and intentional on God's part. In addition we might specifically resist having parts added to us if we cannot see their value.

Unfortunately that is not always the language we pull out of our prophetic promises. Our tendency is to pull out the elements which speak about our importance and singular or unique purpose. We look at Words not as what God will accomplish through our lives but what we ought to do with our lives. Then we try to fulfill the Word by looking for roles equal to the grandeur of the 'promise'. Yet this singular interpretation falls far short of the full picture. If we do not deal with our isolationist perspective we may never allow the necessary preparation given as part of the promise.

The Shared Nature of Destiny

This brings us to the heart of this chapter. Not only do we often misunderstand the process leading to our purpose, but we usually miss the corporate perspective. That is, when God speaks He envisions a people functioning together as one. Let me give you an example.

Many years ago a young man moved to my city. His father knew me and so encouraged him to connect with me. As we spoke on the phone he shared his passion to see more unity in the church of the city. I resonated with his desire. Since I was already part of a group of city leaders who were seeking the Lord and walking together, I instinctively connected with his heart.

He then explained how the Lord had spoken to him and sent him to the city to accomplish this mission. Instead of joining with those who were already walking together with this same desire, he asked if I could begin helping him call leaders together. He wanted to start his own movement of unity in the city. This is a classic misinterpretation of the Word of God. At that moment, I do not think it dawned on him that this was not something the Spirit of God was calling him to lead, but it was something he was called to be part of. Being in unity automatically requires others but does not necessarily call for others to be subordinate.

We often misunderstand directives to participate as mandates to lead. In this case the very nature of unity requires widespread participation. When the Spirit of God calls us to build unity it begins by being in unity and not necessarily creating another movement. Birthing another movement is tantamount to division as now you have competing 'unity' movements. This is the very contradiction of the call to build unity.

In a similar manner the rod is part of an engine. It neither leads an engine nor is it the most vital component. When it finds its place it works nicely as part of a larger vision. On its own it is relatively useless.

When we go back to the Prophetic Word it becomes clear there is a larger context. So for example when the exhortation says, 'I will move you to shift people from one place to another' the Spirit is addressing the entire function of a vehicle with the engine as a significant part. If a rod were to attempt to do this it would only lead to a lifetime of frustration. Frustration which will usually be directed at other believers, who are not recognizing or cooperating with God's unique call on our lives.

Unfortunately this is the place many believers find themselves today. Yet they cannot figure out what is wrong. Having done everything they know to do, they find themselves incapable of making any headway. Unresolved, there is sure to be discouragement and disillusionment.

A Key Revelation

Years ago while I was in the midst of a critical shift in my life I was given a prophetic experience. This moment provided a key insight into my own misunderstanding of the Prophetic Words in my life.

As it happened I was needing to hear God about a move that would affect both my family and ministry. It unfolded in a meeting of leaders from across Canada as we were preparing to receive a significant political leader. A group of about 40 of us were gathered when during the meeting I had the closest thing to an open vision possible. It was so vivid and yet I only saw it with the eyes of my spirit.

The vision unfolded like an illustration for an Encyclopedia I had often read as a child. It was an illustration of a man's anatomy which included the skeletal system, internal organs, muscular system and outermost epidermis. Fascinated as a young boy by human anatomy, I would often look at this illustration in an effort to comprehend myself.

The graphic image consisted of layers of cellophane sheets, each depicting a layer of the body. It began with the human skeleton by itself. Then you could turn down an overlapping translucent page of the internal organs. I cannot remember how many times I had turned these pages up and down mesmerized by the complexity but perfect alignment of our frame. The next sheet included the intricacies of the muscular system which again aligned perfectly.

In this same way my vision unfolded. Sheets seemed to fall from heaven revealing three different layers of prophetic destiny. The first seemed to contain images I recognized representing every single Prophetic Word I had ever received. This in itself was overwhelming and underscores a complexity of God beyond comprehension. Yet, I felt and saw all of them in an instant.

Then a second sheet fell, merging in perfect symmetry with the first. This one carried the sum of

all the collective aspects of what God was
our nation. If that seems unlikely I conc
impossibility of seeing this in a glimpse is ve
beyond myself or any of us. Neverthe ...ss it
unfolded. What was peculiar was the sense in which
some of my personal Words suddenly merged with
these.

This was a defining moment for me. While I was
very much focused on the intention of the vision my
mind registered how often I had misread the
prophetic. I realized in that fleeting moment how
easily I had personally owned Words which in fact
were equally shared by others. It was in this
awareness that I was struck by the exclusive manner
in which I interpreted great purposes I could never
individually bring to birth. It was humbling yet
enlightening.

As though that were not enough to fathom,
another sheet fell which represented the destiny of
the Church I presently pastor. Having been invited
to become the senior leader, my wife and I were in
the throws of discovering the mind of God. While
the offer presented certain benefits it seemed to be
in the opposite direction of everything I understood
God was calling me to in the nations. However in
this church's DNA was something intrinsic to both
Canada's and my destiny. It was a perfect match!

The Outcome

My takeaway gave me an enlarged understanding of the nature of Prophetic Words and Prophetic Purpose. Significant of course, was the limited manner in which I viewed interpreted prophecy. It gave me a fresh desire to abandon my individualistic approach. It is not that there are not personal applications, but only in hindsight do we ever get the larger picture.

When we hear God speaking we must always keep in mind we *'see through a glass dimly'*. What we often hear is His heart for something. It is not necessarily the mandate to be a quarterback, sole initiator or central leader. Often we might be being called to simply participate in something others will lead.

It takes humility and more importantly a macro view of the Kingdom of God to think this way. But like the rod in the engine we are one part of a larger machinery. Though we are being 'used to move people...', as revealed in the prophecy, we are not doing this individually but collectively. May God give us a wider perspective, so we can properly interpret the promises we hope to see fulfilled in our lives.

Chapter 5

The Timelessness of God

A central challenge surrounding the interpretation of Prophetic Ministry has to do with timing. The most common error is made when we attempt to determine precise times and seasons. Both Prophets and recipients alike are prone to misread the time frames of the Holy Spirit. We typically err on the side of optimism, rarely giving enough time for Words to be fulfilled. There is a good reason for this. It has something to do with the timelessness of God.

God is Timeless

One of the most common features of a Prophetic Word is what I call the sense of imminence. This is the unmistakable feeling that one is presently entering the time of fulfillment. It creates the belief that the Word given is on the very verge of coming to pass. Suddenly the recipient is overcome with the impending sense it will all unravel within hours or days. Not only does this add to frustration as the promise is deferred, it can also add a dimension of confusion or doubt as to the certainty of the promise itself. This can be easily alleviated by understanding the mechanics behind the release of a Prophetic Word.

Prophetic ministry is uncovering an important element of the spirit realm. It has to do with the timeless nature of God Himself and the nature of a prophetic moment. When we are receiving a Prophetic Word, a window is being opened into the realm of the eternal. Imagine opening a window in the middle of winter. The atmosphere of the outdoors comes pouring into your house. Similarly the atmosphere of heaven, or at least a touch of it, is flooding in around you during the ministry. You are being engulfed in a world untouched and situated above time.

We get to taste the way God thinks. There is conflict though, since God is not limited the way we are. For God there is really no past, present or future, at least in the sense that we understand it.

All the events unfolding in history are simultaneous, essentially coexisting with Him. In Him everything is Now!

The best way I can describe it is to think of the perspective one might have in a plane. The cars far below are making their way along the twisting roads. They are able to see no more than a mile or so in front of themselves, depending on the terrain. From the sky however, we can see their future destinations now. What they are going to come into can be seen though they are still far from it. It is an imperfect illustration, but points to how God views time.

This is why we can safely say Jesus was crucified before the foundation of the earth.

> *"And all that dwell upon the earth shall worship him, whose names are not written in the book of life of the Lamb slain from the foundation of the world."*
> (Revelation 13:8)

Because time is a construct of God, He is not subject to it. Time is the box God looks into but is not limited by.

NOW Faith Is!

For all intents and purposes everything is Now with God. I once heard a great sermon on this theme. It was based on a Hebrews passage pointing to the ever present nature of faith. The passage focuses on the fact that faith shares attributes that are part of God and therefore reaches outside of time. It reads:

> *"Now faith is the substance of things hoped for, the evidence of things not seen. For by it the elders obtained a good report."*
> (Hebrews 11:1)

This verse points to how faith sees what is not there as though it is there. But more than this it intimates the timeless nature of faith. It is a bit of a word twist but means exactly what is said, which is this: "Now faith is", or "Faith... is now." Faith sees and is convinced of what has not appeared because it steps out of time and into the simultaneous perspective of God.

It is worth noting that it is not coincidental that this faith moment occurs around a 'Word' being given. That is the Prophetic Word not only imparts vision, but it creates faith at the same time. Remember, faith is the product of hearing a Word (Romans 10:17). Faith gives us an ability found in the nature of God. It empowers us to operate in the creative way God does, who is defined as One *"who gives life to the dead and calls those things which do not exist as though they did"* (Romans 4:17).

So when we begin to function in faith we begin to call things into being, but more than that, we step into a timeless world. When I was first introduced to the concept, the preacher kept emphasizing, 'Faith is always now'. By its very nature it is timeless because it is part of the nature of God. God Himself operates by faith. He believes and therefore speaks. When we are in the proximity of this kind of faith we become assured of the same things.

A Testimony

At the very outset of my own training I was struggling to be obedient in the area of finances. I soon discovered trying to believe and believing, are very different things. While God had already spoken to my lack of faith I was determined to stop striving. Laughable really! Yet, as the circumstances and pressures of looming bills drew near the anxiety was eating me up.

Practically speaking we were at the point where we needed almost one thousand dollars to stay afloat. Now bear in mind my ministry calling and gifting were not in question and there were enough key leaders affirming this at the time. I say that simply to indicate I was not just being irresponsible.

However God had restrained my hand from providing for myself and made it very clear I was to believe Him. This was tremendously difficult. I was writing and publishing at the time and, while we had some regular support, it was not enough. Much later I understood that during this time the Lord was training me. He was attempting to convince me of the power of faith and the vanity of striving.

One fateful night it came to a head. Burdened by my growing obligations I wrestled with unbelief and fear. The weight of my circumstances became too great to ignore and clearly I was not making any headway in terms of my faith. While my wife and new baby slept I agonized in prayer over the circumstances, knowing full well 'nothing is impossible to him that believes'. This meant I was the weak link here. I simply did not know how to believe.

But it is in this process that unbelief dies and faith emerges. Somehow I reached this point late that night and crossed over into actual believing. The confidence which entered me was astounding. I knew it was done! Immediately I envisioned someone driving up with a cheque to meet the need and so sat out on my step until one in the morning. No one came but I was filled with assurance. It was not hopeful, I simply knew. Faith is now!

While nothing happened before I went to bed, it was finished. The next day a cheque came in the mail for nine hundred and some random dollars. Literally almost one thousand. It was then that I saw the difference between hopeful optimism and faith. Faith sees and is assured because though it was not in my hands it was done.

Wrapping Up

Faith has an ability to bridge time and leap over the absence of the answer. It gives us the ability to touch a realm without time so that the gap between promise and supply are inconsequential. Obviously, the longer the time gap the more complex the issue. Consider Abraham waiting 25 years without fainting.

The problem arises when the actual time exceeds our faith. But there is a solution to postponed answers. The mistake we make is using the sense of imminence to bind God into our timeline. We can easily begin to set a timetable for the fulfillment of the promise based on our impending sense when we first begin to believe. This is a mistake! The Word is timeless before God but has been appointed a definitive place in time. This means we must exercise both faith and patience to obtain a promise. At least that is how the champions of faith did it.

> *"And we desire that each one of you show the same diligence so as to realize the full assurance of hope until the end, so that you will not be sluggish, but imitators of those who through faith and patience inherit the promises."*
> (Hebrews 6:11-12)

Patience is required particularly because the feeling of imminence has been experienced. Now the challenge becomes bridging these two worlds — a challenge we can deal with more specifically in a future chapter. For now, let's summarize what it means to experience the timelessness of God.

The Word which is 'Now' in the realm where God lives, may yet be years away in the box we call time. That timeless sense with every Prophetic Word makes it feel like it is immediately upon us. But this is just a feature of it coming from a place where there is no time. In the next two chapters we will look at how to continually exercise faith while dealing with the challenge of a delayed promise.

Chapter 6

Contending for the Promise

Once we understand the timelessness of the Prophetic Word there still remains actual fulfillment. What do we do once we receive a promise or Prophetic Word of some type? Many become passive. They adopt a waiting posture, naively hoping the fact that once God has expressed His will, this alone assures completion. Yet, we are instructed to pray *'Your Kingdom come, Your will be done'*. Why pray if God's will is always automatically done?

The Mandate to Contend

The typical stance most people take after they have received a promise is passive. We get excited about the Word as it imparts a sense of God's love for us. The energy of those initial moments can be thrilling and assuring. But then comes delay! We are told to be patient. But is patience just waiting? The answer is No! There is a waiting of sorts, but like everything in the Kingdom this kind of waiting is active. The most comprehensive term to define it is— contend. We must fight for the promises to come to pass. Here are some examples.

The scripture gives us Elijah as the most obvious example of contending. He receives the go ahead from God that the drought is going to end and prophesies as much. But the series of events which follow are odd. Here is what he tells Ahab.

> *"And Elijah said to Ahab, 'Get you up, eat and drink; for there is a sound of abundance of rain.'"*
> (1 Kings 18:41)

Elijah hears the sound of abundance of rain. Presumably it is effectively done; the promise is fulfilled. Yet while he sends Ahab home he himself adopts an entirely different posture. We know it well.

Rather than going to his own home he begins to contend for the promise. He prays by casting himself to the ground and *'put his face between his knees'* (1 Kings 18:42). Then, as he is contending, his servant is sent seven times to see if anything is happening. Only on the seventh time does the servant see any evidence. The point is that despite the promise there was still a process. In this case we do not know how long it took only that Ahab had still not yet left, upon which he was told to make haste.

Timothy

Paul, Timothy's spiritual father, gives him an admonition to contend for his promises. These promises were actually Prophetic Words which the elders spoke over him. Evidently a team had ministered and prophesied to Timothy with the laying on of hands, that he would accomplish certain things. No specifics are given, but the Words spoken did indeed have to do with his calling. Again, like with Elijah, the promises are not automatic.

> *"This command I entrust to you, Timothy, my son, in accordance with the prophecies previously made concerning you, that <u>by them you fight the good fight</u>,"*
> (1 Timothy 1:18)

So while he is encouraged to press into the destiny outlined by the Prophetic Words, he is told to use those Prophetic Words to do it, *"... by them fight..."*. This is vital! Remember the Word of God is a sword. It is a two-edged sword designed to be used for warfare both in our own selves and against all that would resist the promise.

Not Automatic

The mistake we make all too often is believing if God said it then it will all just happen. No! No! No! The promises must be fought for and planted and nurtured in our hearts with deliberate action. Just as Timothy must fight for the reality of his destiny, so must we. We must, like any warrior, take the sword and battle with it.

Swords are designed for battle and so the Word of promise you receive is a weapon. It is no coincidence that this truth is featured also in the book of Hebrews, at the very point where the reader is being encouraged to conquer unbelief. The operative word being–conquer. It is not by accident that this book is all about apprehending the promise.

"For the word of God is living and powerful, and sharper than any two-edged sword, piercing even to the division of soul and spirit, and of joints and marrow, and is a discerner of the thoughts and intents of the heart."

(Hebrews 4:12)

It is time to take our swords and contend. Mere waiting is a passive stance not reflective of true faith. Sometimes this passivity can leave us with a latent benign promise. These like seeds never planted have a future potential but are powerless to move ahead.

A Sad End

This was my experience when I was asked to pray for a man dying of cancer. He was a faithful member of the church I was in and seemed to have a vibrant faith. He and his wife were integral to the congregation and from my perspective he was certainly a good Christian.

As I went to his home to pray he demonstrated all the signs of faith. He was expectant of a miracle and talked about unfulfilled promises in his life. He believed he could not die as his time was not done. Pointing to various Prophetic Words about ministry and specific events which had not yet happened, he declared his conviction. I believed he had faith to be healed. Remembering the scripture which declares *'all things are possible to him that believes'* I expected him to live. He did not.

I was surprised and disappointed. The energy in his conversation had led me to believe he was faithfully waiting for these things to unfold. This was part of the problem. As I prayed in my frustration over his passing, the Lord began to speak to me about the conditions for answered prayer and prophetic promises. It was then that I determined to discover God's heart for me. It was a tragic end for a life lived with such expectation of promises. However, for me, it was the beginning of a new pursuit — a search. This search has led me on a hunt for scriptures which define our role in obtaining promises.

Fortunately I did not have to look very far as those who have gone before us were met with similar frustrations and questions. The admonitions of the Book of Hebrews has become a significant resource in this quest. It has become obvious the Lord has not left us without clear guidelines. In the next two chapters we will look more closely at the process God intends us to follow in pursuit of our promises.

Chapter 7

Entering the Promise 1.1

Believers often make mistakes when determining the validity of a particular Word. Waiting to see whether the promise comes to pass is a common one. While there are certain Words designed to simply unfold over time, many require our active participation. Without this participation the Word is dormant. To passively wait shows a clear misunderstanding of how the prophetic is meant to work. Certainly we must decide whether a Word is for us or not, but we cannot stop there. Like Elijah, we must contend for the Words we believe to be true. But how we contend is the question needing an answer.

Facing a Similar Struggle

This is perhaps the most neglected and misunderstood element of the prophetic. When it comes to interpreting and handling a Prophetic Word many promises are lost because they are not incubated correctly. Like seeds held but never planted, nothing ever comes of them. Fortunately there is a distinct Biblical pattern left to us by the Apostle Paul and others. This template gives us a path we can follow in order to inherit the promises.

Struggle is very often a necessary part of the process. Just because it is challenging does not mean it is not God. The need to contend for the promise is not a reflection of our failure. Rather it may reflect the fact that we are maturing and entering into a place of being co-workers with God.

Indeed just as the 1st century church struggled with this very issue, so should we. The instruction they received is equally valid for us today as it was for them. The bulk of this advice was given in Hebrews.

This book primarily addresses the challenges of our pursuit of God's promises. It is written to a people who were losing hope on account of delay. Life was not unfolding as was promised or expected. In their case, persecution and extreme circumstances were causing them to grow weary. In the midst of their trials they began to question, 'Was any of this real?' The encouragement given them, is now for us.

The writer begins by citing the quest of the ancient Hebrews whose journey is well chronicled. Many of them failed along the way. Through their failure he gives them, and us, definitive keys. Their physical journey from Egypt into their promised land is a literal version of our metaphorical effort to obtain the promises God has given us. His encouragement was also a warning to keep them from falling into the same trap their forefathers did. In so doing we are given the very means to contend for our promises and, at the same time, it reveals the reasons some did not enter.

To state it plainly the primary reason for failure is unbelief. This should not shock any of us. Our entire life in Christ is a quest to grow in faith. We should never recoil at the idea that we all struggle on some level with unbelief. Growing faith will always be part of our journey.

This means we do not have to feel condemned for failing to believe. However, we should do something about it otherwise the results will be the same as those coming out of Egypt who did not believe.

Mixing It With Faith

In fact this is the very reason the author of the book of Hebrews gives them this warning. He is teaching them the dynamics of believing. While we would do well to review the entirety of the book of

Hebrews let's begin with some key verses. The end of chapter three clearly declares Israel could not inherit their promise because of unbelief. We cannot gloss over this fact.

> *"And to whom did He swear that they would not enter His rest, but to those who did not obey? So we see that they could not enter in because of unbelief."*
> (Hebrews 3:18-19)

We cannot overemphasize this point. Unbelief is the root cause of disobedience. Leaders are often afraid to challenge their followers regarding this point, however it is clear from both here and other passages. Furthermore we have this stalwart principle from Jesus Himself telling us, *'nothing is impossible to him who believes'* (Matthew 19:26, Mark 9:23). Nothing is impossible if we believe. This should inspire us to own our journey.

But, this is where the writer gets even more specific. He points to the risk before them, to the point of telling them to... get this...FEAR. How is that for oxymoronic?

> *"Therefore, since a promise remains of entering His rest, let us <u>fear</u> lest any of you seem to have come short of it. For indeed the <u>gospel was preached</u> to us as well as to them; but the word which they*

heard __did not profit__ them, __not being__
__mixed with faith__ in those who heard it."
(Hebrews 4:1-2)

What does it mean to fear in this sense? What he is really saying is plainly, *'be forewarned and attentive to this'*. But, more importantly, do the following. The key part we want to focus on is what they omitted. The word they heard *'did not profit them'* because they failed to do something... mix it with faith!

Now we should remember that the writer is using the Old Testament experience of Israel to encourage the new believers. He was telling them to press forward and obtain their promises. His warning was to say, *'Israel did not enter their promise but you can enter yours'*. It is critical for us to know the very same dynamics are in play for us.

These, like us today, were given a prophetic promise. The message of hope or the 'gospel' was **preached** to them. This is worth remembering! That is, through Moses and Joshua, God spoke or preached to them. They heard God's Word but they did not follow through. This meant though they heard, it did not benefit them since it was not mixed with faith. It is the 'mixing' with faith element we need to look at.

Patience

However before we go into the whole process of this we should be reminded of one other key factor, which is the role of 'patience'. We are reminded of the precedent for how men of old received their promises.

> *"And we desire that each one of you show the same diligence to the full assurance of hope until the end, that you do not become sluggish, but imitate those who through faith and patience inherit the promises."*
> (Hebrews 6:11-12)

So men of old were required to inherit the promise through the exercise of both faith and patience. We must apply the same diligence. We should understand that both elements are necessary.

Patience is the 'waiting' component. It suggests the passing of time. But what does it mean to mix it with faith? Let me start by saying it does not mean just waiting. This is critical to understand so let us repeat it. Mixing with faith is not synonymous with mere waiting. Sometimes we can enter a prolonged waiting period without doing the mixing of faith. Patience is great, but without the active ingredient of faith, patience will only produce endless waiting. This is a passive default we commonly succumb to when we really do not believe. In the end it makes our hearts sick.

The posture of faith is something else entirely. When we resolve to 'hold on', we are just "not quitting" but that is all. This amounts to waiting... then waiting longer... then waiting more. That is not the intention God had when He gave us the promise. Instead, we are called to a certain kind of action.

The truth is the enemy is at work all the time, stealing and destroying. He is trying to usurp our faith and promises. We have an opportunity to set in motion spiritual forces which will cause destiny to unfold. Let's take the initiative. In the next chapter we will explore the practical way we can stand in faith. The second part of Entering the Promise will unveil the real heart of a life of faith.

Chapter 8

Entering the Promise 1.2

To really understand how to contend we have to turn to the book of Romans. While the specific steps are mentioned in Hebrews they are not as concrete as what Paul tells us in Romans. Paul, in this book, is far more explicit and gives us a detailed plan for releasing faith and appropriating promises. That is what contending is really about. Not just waiting but mixing faith with the promise while exercising patience.

The Act of Believing

The mechanics of real faith are explained in Romans 10. Paul gives us a very clear synopsis of how to enact faith. In particular, He explains the way faith works when you become born again. This is important to understand. Why? Because the same steps that apply to the promise of salvation feature equally with all other promises. In other words, the way faith works to get you saved is the way faith works to get you anything from God.

Here is Paul's primary thesis:

> **"But what does it say? 'The word is near you, in your mouth and in your heart' (that is, the word of faith which we preach): that if you confess with your mouth the Lord Jesus and believe in your heart that God has raised Him from the dead, you will be saved. For with the heart one believes unto righteousness, and with the mouth confession is made unto salvation."**
> (Romans 10:8-10)

Paul is giving us an antidote for obtaining a promise. It is composed of two essential parts. The first is believing in our hearts and the second has to do with speaking. Consider! With the heart we believe unto righteousness. This is great but the second part is equally important. *'With the mouth confession is made unto salvation'*. The righteousness part is what gets you into heaven, but the salvation part is what changes you on earth.

Now let's remember where we are! The Hebrews are discouraged because they are not inheriting their promises. Things are seemingly going the opposite of what they thought. So they are reminded of Israel who fainted and did not enter their promise. Again the reason is, they did not exercise faith, that is they did not believe. They needed to mix faith with the promise. This requires the entire two-step process, which is believing in the heart but then confessing with the mouth. They had to speak! Inheriting a promise involves contending by using your mouth and your sound. Instead of 'interpreting' the promise as a 'wrong prophecy', we are told to contend.

My Experience

By the grace of God I stumbled into discovering some of these things years ago. In my early attempts to obey God, I began our ministry and I felt strongly that I was uniquely called to walk by faith. The details are many but I was restrained from doing typical things a pastor or ministry might be allowed to do. Every time I stepped beyond my mandate I was sternly rebuked with the words, 'I never told you to do that.' I was attempting to follow conventional wisdom, but apparently God was not interested in conventional ministry.

Little did I know, but I was in God's University. I was to discover the essence of genuine faith by discovering what it was not. It began with Prophetic Words I received in abundance. There were so many I cannot remember them all, but they largely had to do with my call and provision which would follow. Like most other believers in training I did not know how to contend and stumbled at this point. Like most I waited!

Before long it became clear the promises were not coming to pass. At least not in the time frame I had anticipated.

Perhaps because of need, I was focused on supply for my family, as well as the expansion of influence God had promised. We were living but just barely. I believed the promises given me but I was waiting. To encourage myself I would read and reread the Words of various prophets, sometimes listening to recordings.

I remembered the promises but was frustrated by the seeming delay. When those Words came through the mouth of ministers I had felt the imminence of them. This is the dynamic I shared in an earlier chapter on timelessness. The sense of imminence felt and sounded like they were about to cascade into my life. They did not! Weeks passed and then months. I would be discouraged and then encouraged by another Word from yet another prophet. 'How long?', I wondered!

In the midst of these days something began to unfold. It happened that while living in the Vancouver area I would routinely pick up our mail both at home and across the border in Blaine Washington. Approaching the mailboxes was a matter of both optimism and dread. Usually there was some financial crisis looming.

I vividly remember approaching with a sense of hope. This was fuelled by the fact that I believed in the promises and felt I had waited long enough. In addition, some larger ministries had published some of my writings and I received great feedback from some key leaders. Still, more times than not, I was greeted with an empty box, or worse, a hand full of bills. The weight of hopelessness was suffocating. Sometimes it was all I could do to not meltdown on the spot, and with great heaviness I would walk back to my car.

It was beyond my capacity, yet I had nowhere to turn. I believed enough that I could not go back and yet, seemingly, I was powerless to move forward. Little did I know He wanted me to go up!

The Upward Journey

Sitting in my vehicle surrounded by a cloud of darkness I would boil with frustration. Yet I knew if I let this cloud infect me I would lose hope entirely. The oppressive atmosphere strangled me to the point where I knew I could not stay immobile.

Instinctively I knew I must lift myself out of the hopelessness engulfing my soul. So I did the only thing I knew to do.

Having discovered early in my walk how to escape depression and the overwhelming feelings of discouragement, I would begin to pray out loud in the Spirit. It seemed the only thing I could do as it was impossible to formulate any positive thoughts of my own. Praying in tongues was the only thing I could do. As it turns out it was the best thing to do.

Now I had previously discovered the most effective way to use this tool and so I simply did what I always did. This involved praying out loud and deliberately to the point of aggression. In some earlier moments of desperation in my life, it became clear that shutting out other voices by expending this concerted effort was critical. Also, speaking out loud so as to hear my own voice helped overcome fear and created an atmosphere of faith.

This principle had brought me through a number of key challenges before this time. It was after about 10 to 15 minutes that the atmosphere would begin to shift and hope would strengthen me. Fear and anxiety would give way to confidence and hope. Without any other alternatives, this is what I did while I sat in the car, far too discouraged to drive, or do anything else really.

MARC BRISEBOIS

In the Spirit

This transition is vital to comprehend. At the time I did not realize what I was doing, but in the spirit realm I was navigating to a place of promise. It is an upward journey. In terms of what I was experiencing however, you have to realize there was no desire to pray and there was no optimism at all, only paralyzing fear. It was only the knowledge that my faith could die in this place that made me pray. Like a drowning man I furiously fought my way upward in order to breathe.

Then the darkness would begin to crack. Like light piercing the dusk of night, something of God's beauty would enter the moment and I would begin to soar. Scriptures suddenly jumped into my consciousness declaring the faithfulness of God. Within another 10 minutes I would begin shouting and declaring aloud the promises I had always known to be true, but which had faded in the reality of today. It was not really emotional as much as it was raw inevitability.

Without realizing it, I was returning to the place I had been when the promises were first given. It was like getting another Word except it was the same Word renewed. The same optimism and imminence penetrated my heart as though the prophets were shouting their promises into my ears and heart. Again, I was freshly filled with the sense these promises were coming upon me. I knew the answer was coming. Maybe not this very second, but very,

71

very soon. What was happening is, I was recreating the moment when the prophets gave me the promise.

When someone prophesies over you they are not only receiving a Word from God, but also from a place. That place is where you are supposed to be seated (Ephesians 1:21). The place then is as important as the promise. Like plants that grow better in their native soil, a promise blooms in the land from which it was birthed.

By pressing upward in prayer I was returning to the place of the promise. In that place the Word comes alive again and faith springs from my heart. Like the first moment when the prophet spoke we are experiencing the Word of God but without the aid of a prophet. This is the action of faith. The result was that I was refreshed with the same imminent expectation as when God initially spoke.

The process of declaring out loud was a mixing of faith. It causes us to transcend time. Remember? Faith is always now. As such, there is no waiting and the sense of delay disappears as another NOW moment compels me to know I am standing in my destiny. Though I cannot see it with my natural eyes, it has become as real as anything. This is the cure for deferred hope. It is the only way a man like Abraham can wait 25 years without losing the vision of the promise.

Faith

Faith allows your future to be experienced in the present. It effectively reaches into the future and pulls the promise into your NOW moment. This gives a sense of assurance. Rather than just waiting, you are virtually handling the promise. It is tangible and real.

This works because it gives you an ability to see as God sees, which is part of the reward of faith. When you walk this way both future and past are Now. This is part of why Paul says we are *seated in heavenly places* (Ephesians 2:6). There is a heavenly perspective we have been invited to participate in which is part of our inheritance. Now we do not always function from this place, but it is where and how He foreordained us to operate. That is, as children and heirs of God, we are seated in a realm unaffected by time; we can SEE the promise fulfilled.

One can see the wisdom of God at work in this entire process. He locks us into a place where we cannot make the promise come to pass and yet we are unwilling to retreat. Then through our faith born of desperation, He makes a way where there is no way. It is neither forward nor back - it is up. Meaning instead of moving like we might normally do in our life's journey, He calls us higher.

We experience the freedom of faith by ascending. In my journey I had ascended to the place where my promise was born. It is the same place from which prophets and faith speak: near the throne of God where time is no longer a factor.

And so contending for the promise makes it new again. Instead of seeking someone to once again prophesy, we are ascending to the Word as it is continually before God. This is mixing the promise with faith. Too often and without knowing it, we do not exercise faith and instead lean on someone else's ministry gift. It is far easier to use the surrogate faith of a prophetic ministry than it is to actually believe. So rather than ascending to the promise, we want yet another Word to create that glorious confidence we first felt.

But we do not need to wait to see the validity of a promise by whether it comes to pass. Rather:

> **"But what does it say? 'The word is near you, in your mouth and in your heart, that is, the word of faith which we preach:'"**
> (Romans 10:8)

Our salvation is close at hand.

Chapter 9

Managing your Future Self

The final phase of nurturing a Prophetic Word brings us to a natural conclusion–the fulfilled promise. How do you know if you are there? Some are easier to see than others. If you are believing for a car, it is simple to know if you have it. However, prophetic ministry often touches less specific parts of destiny. In these cases we need to be more discerning how Words apply to us. Still, even in this, the Holy Spirit has provided answers.

Prophetic Gauges?

The outcome of some promises are easier to gauge than others. The markers for ambiguous issues like influence or other ministry characteristics are not always clear. These are more likely to tie into thresholds not easily substantiated. For example we might be looking for a degree of maturity in our gifting or a breadth of authority promised to us. Sometimes we have a Word about a kind of person we are becoming and the natural consequences of that transformation. In these cases we need to avoid premature expectations. Especially those which demand some kind of recognition from others.

There is a challenge innate to maturity itself. Because God is ultimately interested in purifying our hearts we must exercise careful impatience. Too often when we receive a Word about 'Who' we are going to become, we assume we are almost there. That presumption can lead to having expectations from others. That is, we can assume to be treated in the present for who we are going to be in the future. This was a challenge for me personally.

In my case I received numerous Words about influence and a breadth of ministry. It included the fact God was going to give me 'widespread' favour in nations. However, many times along the way I wondered why others were slow to recognize my role. There was a good reason.

It has everything to do with the difference between a seed and a full grown tree. The seed does not feel less than a tree and yet it is. It is a captive of its future self because it has the DNA of a full grown tree, and in the Spirit there is no time. Even though it is only a seed it feels like a tree. Yet, it has never been a tree and so it cannot know the difference between the seed (DNA) and a fully mature tree.

This is in essence one of our great challenges as we wait for DNA (seed) to bring us into Destiny (tree). The DNA is important because it tells us who we really are, however we still live in time and must not try to escape this reality. We struggle gauging the gulf separating these two. The tension is between who I am (seed) and who I am meant to be (tree). The seed of destiny shouts as though it were full grown and our sense of the future does the same.

Vague Language

Complicating this process is the nature of language itself, which we have already hinted at. My interpretation of words like 'widespread' can be arbitrary while the Holy Spirit had His own intent. Remember the admonition given about how we use the Word of God.

> *"knowing this first, that no prophecy of Scripture is of any private interpretation, for prophecy never came by the will of man, but holy men of God*

spoke as they were moved by the Holy Spirit."
(2 Peter 1:20)

The point is we cannot make a Word mean what we want it to mean. There can be no private interpretation, meaning only the intention of the Holy Spirit matters.

Usually when we receive promises like this the language can be pretty vague. There is no glossary of terms we can use to verify our thoughts. As with this Word in particular there are various levels of 'widespread' available. You can spread butter on a piece of bread so large the butter is barely detectable. It is still widespread but may not exactly be what you were thinking. By the same token, having influence on twenty people in each of 100 nations is also an example of widespread influence. What is God's intent and how can I know I have arrived?

Part of interpreting the prophetic is being earnestly committed to the original intent of the Holy Spirit. It is far too easy to read into Prophetic Words like 'widespread influence'–things we wish to hear. The widespread influence of a Billy Graham or Reinhard Bonnke, for example, will be rare. So what kind of influence did God intend when you received a promise? The range of possibilities is truly great.

Proofs

At the end of the day we are looking for outside proofs to ensure our expectations are reasonable and match our actual purpose. Like sports, there are tiers to every promise. Our aspirations must match the intended league the Holy Spirit was indicating. How can we know?

The ultimate proof is always found in the fulfillment itself. Eventually the proof of our role will become evident in our function. Like the proverb which says 'water finds its own level', for us it means the intent of God is more important than our expectation. Humility is critically necessary to accept the measure God intended. Impatience can balk at the pace at which these things are unfolding, but a sincere and pure heart will want to think 'soberly'. Again Paul reminds us:

"For I say, through the grace given to me, to everyone who is among you, not to think of himself more highly than he ought to think, but to think soberly, as God has dealt to each one a measure of faith."
(Romans 12:3)

This is critical for our state of mind along the way. It also might determine whether or not others can live with us during our process.

Despite the faith needed to step into our future we need to have a realistic sense of who we are in the moment. It reminds me of a time I was in Bible School and went out to play for the hockey team. Someone asked me if I was any good. Not really knowing the calibre of the others I said I was 'ok'. When I asked him the same question he responded saying he was great. It became clear on the ice that his claim did not match his skills. He had an unrealistic view of his abilities with respect to others in this league. When walking out the metron of our journey we must realize that it will be obvious what our true measure is. At least to those who can truly see.

Rather than imposing our hopes on God and His people around us, we need to get trustworthy feedback. This requires we watch for the evidence from others. The response we consistently receive from others, especially from mature fathers and mothers, tells us how far our journey has taken us.

For example, if you are called to be a powerful prophet it is not necessary to convince others. If it has become true others will tell you. The litmus test that we are actually stepping into fulfillment is so self-evident, it is easy for others to see. Too often, we will fault others for not being able to detect how amazing we have become.

Without Honour

It is perhaps wise to add an important extension to these thoughts by revisiting something Jesus said. One of the most frequent errors in this arena has been with prophetic people who overestimate their stature. Unfortunately, this is at least part of the reason that many have been wary of prophetic ministry. While, granted, there is a key faith component, apprehending a promise is important to merging our future selves with our current self.

The prophetic ministry is not an excuse for denial. Sometimes our patience gives way to frustration and we jump ahead of ourselves. It usually will result in trying to use a promise yet in our future, to convince others about the present. But what we are becoming is never achieved at the expense of who we are now. Again, the perspective of people around us can be an important gauge as to whether we have begun to apprehend the promises God has given us.

When we are prone to ignore the evidence we usually use this convenient verse.

> *"But Jesus, said unto them, 'A prophet is not without honour, but in his own country, and among his own kin, and in his own house.'"*
> (Mark 6:4)

Of course in so doing we ignore an important aspect of what Jesus said. He said, *a prophet is not without honour*. '*Not without*' means a true prophet will always *have* honour. This is saying they are recognizable.

He is not saying everyone will reject him, but that close family members who are acquainted with his natural person are sometimes the last to see. But everybody else will notice, which is the point. If only two people recognize your 'stature', and they are new friends from the internet, you might not be there yet. Do not prematurely cry foul! There is no need to jump ahead of where we actually are at the moment.

The Seed

Remember, the essential structure of the kingdom of God is organic. Everything begins as a seed (Luke 8:11, 1 Peter 1:23). When a Prophetic Word is given to you, it is given as a seed planted into the soil of your heart. At this point only the soil knows the promise is there. Nobody else needs to know!

Like the seed in the ground people bypass each and everyday, it is not hindered by their lack of acknowledgment. That is, the affirmation of others cannot really add or take away from your promise, though it can give encouragement. But even then if a seed is over-watered it will spoil. Instead, just as any gardener might do, we must wait patiently for the precious fruit of the earth to rise itself. We will know we are walking in the promise when others begin to see what we have felt for a long time.

If others are not seeing what we feel, we should begin to question it's authenticity.

In this case the value of fathers and mothers in our lives is priceless. They can prophetically see what is in soil and call it forth. Still, we must be willing to live within the sphere God has currently provided.

Final Thoughts

Finally we need to rest in the power of the promise at work inside of us. Having done all we need to stand, trusting God's Word will not return void. Jesus said as much in the parable of the sower. Those who with a good heart receive the seed will produce a harvest. Some more than others (30, 60, 100, Mark 4:20), but the promise will deliver. Like the farmer we must simply guard the harvest and wait patiently for the fruit of the earth (James 5:7).

Chapter 10

The Macro Prophetic Picture

Despite the importance of our individual journeys they all culminate at the same place. That is, there is one promise we all share which should form the pinnacle of our hopes and dreams. This prophetic promise transcends generations and joins to Prophets of Old who sought for a city.

A City

Unfortunately, this is one kind of promise which cannot be apprehended by a single generation. While it will be met by one, it is brought into place by many. It is the unresolvable promise of a Kingdom culminating in the manifestation of a City. While this is on the outer edge of our theme, it points to some promises which stretch across more than one lifetime.

By extension it suggests there are some destinies which are too large for a single 120 year period. Like the fathers before us, we can hold onto it without ever seeing it. Once again the mystery unfolds in the book of Hebrews. It says:

> ***"By faith Abraham obeyed when he was called to go out to the place which he would receive as an inheritance. And he went out, not knowing where he was going. By faith he dwelt in the land of promise as in a foreign country, dwelling in tents with Isaac and Jacob, the heirs with him of the same promise; for he waited for the city which has foundations, whose builder and maker is God"***
> (Hebrews 11:8-10)

Like a chord of many strands woven together Abraham saw a prophetic convergence. His promise was an inheritance he saw but never owned, but it was anchored to a larger picture. In the meantime, he was content to live by faith as a foreigner in the land he was promised. Yet, while his descendants eventually stepped into it, the physical land was secondary in his expectation.

The real focus of his hope was in an Eternal Kingdom coming to earth. He never prayed 'Your Kingdom come on earth as it is in heaven', as far as we know, but this was the essence of his interpretation of the promise. He waited for a city!

It was not just any city as though he pined for a place to live. This city was built by God. Paul spoke of the identical hope as the means to survive the challenges of this present age. *"For we know that if our earthly house, this tent, is destroyed, we have a building from God, a house not made with hands, eternal in the heavens"* (2 Corinthians 5:1). Paul and Abraham focused their faith on a moment which for some would take place after death, but for a privileged few, in the full light of day.

Application

The highest purpose of our faith is not for personal pleasure. Let me illustrate it this way. Early in my journey the Holy Spirit spoke to me about writing. I began to write without realizing the length of days ahead of me. That is, I did not realize the early articles were in themselves relatively pointless except to develop a skill. If I had not valued each and every one, I would not have developed the discipline to continue.

Like an athlete on the practice field repeating a motion again and again, the immediate result is inconsequential. He may or may not enjoy repeatedly kicking a ball. Either way the desired end is not reached at the conclusion of an hour of practice, but over the long run as he applies those skills toward a championship. The true dividends are reaped on gameday in the heat of battle.

Similarly, faith is being tested and perfected in us. It is applied to personal achievements. We apply faith to promises in order to obtain a job, a healing or a ministry. Yet, it is all practice for a much larger goal. A house or a ministry can be promised and delivered in a lifetime, but a Kingdom like the one we look for is forged over countless lifetimes of faith.

For this reason the measure of some promises cannot be that they come to pass. Consider this pivotal passage verifying the faith of those faithful saints of old:

> *"These all died in faith, not having received the promises, but having seen them afar off were assured of them, embraced them and confessed that they were strangers and pilgrims on the earth. For those who say such things declare plainly that they seek a homeland. And truly if they had called to mind that country from which they had come out, they would have had opportunity to return. But now they desire a better, that is, a heavenly country. Therefore God is not ashamed to be called their God, for He has prepared a city for them."*

(Hebrews 11:13-16)

Like Abraham, the promise they prized most was for a city. There is value in obtaining every promise. But like my early articles, divinely designed for practice, they can be a means to an end.

What this means for us is a hierarchy of purpose in the heart of God. While He is deeply committed to seeing our lives prosper He has an endgame for the faith He is forging in you. Interpreting the Prophetic must by definition encompass an appreciation of the bigger picture. Enjoy the abundant life God is bringing you into but realize, we are 'His workmanship' prepared for works which have their final expression beyond one lifetime.

To learn more about Marc Brisebois and Watchman on the Wall Ministries, visit our website at www.watchman.ca.

Marc publishes the "Chronicle" - an online newsletter once every couple of weeks. To join our mailing list, visit www.watchmanchronicle.com. Sign up to receive fresh revelatory insights into the Word of God!

Made in USA - Crawfordsville, IN
66119_9780986829949
10.25.2021 1018